PRINCIPLES TO LIVING HOLY
IN THESE LAST AND EVIL DAYS

I'M SAVED!

NOW WHAT?
SHAVONNE ANDREWS

I'm Saved! Now What?
Published by: Shavonne Andrews
Website: http://www.shavonneandrews.com

Scripture marked KJV are taken from the KING JAMES VERSION (KJV): KING JAMES VERSION, public domain.

This book or parts thereof may not be reproduced in any form, stored in a retrieval system, or transmitted in any form by any means- electronic, mechanical, photocopy, recording, or otherwise-without prior written permission of the publisher, except as provided by United States of America copyright law. Thank you for your support of the author's rights.

Copyright © 2016 by Shavonne Andrews
All Rights reserved

ISBN-13: 978-0-692-74259-4

Printed in the United States of America

This book is available at a special discount when ordered in bulk quantity. Please visit the author's website for more information.

ALEXANDER,

After 11 years and counting, my love for you has never changed.

I love you more than you will ever know.

Thanks for supporting me in everything I do.

CONTENTS

	Introduction	9
1	A Call for Repentance	13
2	I'm Saved! Now What?	35
3	Delivered from Darkness	61
4	A New Beginning	85
5	Talk to God, He's Listening	103
6	A Living Sacrifice	107
7	Activate Your Faith	121
8	Favor in the Storm	127
9	Forever His	133
	Conclusion	143
	Notes	147
	Daily Prayers	157
	A Message From the Author	170

ACKNOWLEDGEMENTS

Special thanks to my sponsors:
my mother Lenora Love,
my sister Mozella Grice,
my aunt Mercilla Cooley,
my cousin Shelby Cooley,
my sister in Christ Sedonte Simmons,
to Prophet R. K. James
and his lovely family,
and to those who supported me through
encouraging words and prayer,
from the bottom of my heart, thank you.
Your generous contribution has helped me
towards the publication of this book.
Because of your support,
many lives will be forever changed.

Introduction

I've found that when you truly love someone, you give your best, you give your last and even give your all. That's the exact kind of love that God has for you. His love is unconditional and He would do any and everything for us all because we are His children and He loves us. The purpose of this book is to fully understand God's love and in return, live our lives as a living sacrifice, holy and acceptable unto Him.

Some may ask, realistically, how is it even possible to fully live for God? Well, it is very much so possible. There was a time in my life when I would completely forget to talk to

God, pray to Him, read His word or even do His will. Even though I was saved, I didn't have a relationship with Him. I had a nine-to-five job working for the bank. I was pregnant and was always tired. I would come home after work to tend to my husband and children by cooking, cleaning, doing laundry, running errands, etc. It got to the point I didn't even have time for me. I would always find myself exhausted and couldn't wait to get into bed and go to sleep. It literally took a very humbling point in my life that brought me closer to God.

About a year ago, I went to a church service one Sunday morning and the message was, "There are people in hell who desires Jesus!" That pastor had my full and undivided attention because I knew that I wasn't where I was supposed to be in God. The message pointed out that there are people in hell who wish they could get another chance, but it's forever too late. They cry out to Jesus day and night but Jesus is saying, "It's too late!" That message touched me in such a way, I knew it was time for a change. That same night, God called on me and I answered. He showed me a dream of me working in the youth ministry at my church and within three months, I was in my church working for the Lord and it all started with me humbling myself. I didn't know how I was going to do it, but I did.

The church was forty-five minutes away from my house. I said, "God I don't know how I'm going to do this, but I love you so much that if this is what you want me to do, Lord I'll do it." So I did. I found myself working in ministry for a year then I was appointed to be a Sunday school teacher for our youth and that's where I am today. God has been so good to me. I am so excited and looking forward to more of what God has in stored for me.

I am so grateful for the gift of life in itself. He has always been there for me and my family. Growing up, we didn't always have much and there were many times we didn't have anything, but because God loved us so much, he always provided and made a way.

The same goes for you. I'm sure you can agree that God has been there for you in so many ways and I bet you can't count all of your blessings on one hand either. Surely, if you are living and breathing then I know He has been good to you. If you can't think of anything, well you can start off by giving God thanks for waking you up this morning. If you are in good health, that's another reason to give God thanks. Maybe some of you reading this book couldn't have children, but God made a way and now you've been blessed with kids. If you know that God has been good to you, just lift your hands and tell Him thank you, because surely He deserves it!

In this book, you will learn how to incorporate God in your everyday life. By implementing what you learn from this book will not teach you how to live the, *Perfect Religious Life,* but how to maintain an ongoing relationship with Jesus, which will prepare you for His return.

CHAPTER 1

A Call for Repentance

I am well aware that people from all over the world are from many different backgrounds, religions and cultures, but what I'm going to share with you has nothing to do with that. In fact, I only want to share with you the love of God and who He is to me. Many people may not believe that He is our creator or maybe never even heard of His unconditional love, but the Bible tells us in the book of John that God loves us so much that He sent His only Son to die on the cross for our sins and anyone who believes in Him shall be saved and live with Him forever.

For God so loved the world that he gave his only begotten son. That whosoever believeth in him shall not perish but have everlasting life.
-John 3:16

Have you ever thought about when your life is over, where you would spend all eternity? Many people don't think about it, some simply don't care and others really just don't know, but I must express my concern to you that where you spend all eternity is very important to me.

For the sake of not assuming that everyone has read the Bible for themselves, I want to show you what took place in the book of Genesis and how it plays such an important role in our everyday lives today. Did you know that in the beginning when Adam and Eve disobeyed God, it effected all of us? The minute they disobeyed God was the minute they became sinners and one of the consequences of their sin was that their children's, children's, children, (which is you and I) would be born into sin. All because Adam and Eve had sinned, all born into this world were born a sinner.

Wherefore, as by one man sin entered into the world, and death by sin; and so death passed upon all men, for that all have sinned.

-*Romans 5:12*

WHAT IS SIN?

Sin is an act of disobedience against God's will or His laws. A separation from God. Literally, we were all born a sinner.

Before Adam and Eve sinned, they once had such an amazing relationship with God because they knew Him personally. When God created Adam and Eve, He had placed them in the Garden of Eden, a place where there was no death, no pain, no sickness, no hatred, no jealously, no lust and there was absolutely no need for anything, because all of their needs were met. Everything was provided for them and the garden was such a perfect place to live. God told them they can eat any fruit they please except for the tree of knowledge of good and evil. When God created man, He created us in His image.

He created us to be holy and acceptable unto Him and He intended for it to be that way forever, but once they disobeyed God that changed everything!

WHAT ARE GOD'S LAWS FOR US?

Because this world is so corrupted and filled with sin, God Word says that He's going to destroy it and everything therein by pouring out His wrath upon the world with fire, but God also says that if we love Him and keep His commandments, not only will He show us mercy for the rest of our days, which includes living a long, blessed and favor-filled life, but we'll also have everlasting life with Him forever.

Now there's no need to fear, because God promises us that those who love Him and keep His commandments will be saved. He assures us that He will destroy this world with fire, but there will be a new heaven and a new earth. So we need to be excited and look forward toward the promises that He has for us. God doesn't ask for too much. All He wants is for us to love Him and keep His commandments, but for those who do not believe in Him and keep His commandments will face the wrath of God.

According to Exodus 20:2-17, God gives Moses laws for us to live by. These laws give us instructions on how to live holy. It tells us that we are not to serve or worship any other false gods, we are not to make, serve or have any idols because God is a jealous God, we are not to take the Lord's name in vain, we're to remember the Sabbath day and keep it holy and we are to honor our fathers and mothers. He says by doing so, our days will be long upon the land.

God also makes it clear that we are not to kill, commit adultery, steal, bear false witness against our neighbors, nor to covet, (meaning to want what others have).

CONSEQUENCES OF SIN
The wages of sin is death.

Ever since sin entered into the world, it's been corrupted with evil and wickedness and the result of it is death. Now just because we were born into sin doesn't mean that we have to be doomed forever. God loves us so much that He sent His only son Jesus Christ to die on the cross for us. By doing so, anyone who believes in Him will be saved.

Do you believe that Jesus Christ died on the cross for your sins? Because He loves you so much, He knew that in order for you to be saved, a sacrifice needed to be made, so He gave up His life. He knew that He was going to have to take the punishment that we should have gotten. Therefore, He was crucified and died for you and I, but on the third day, He rose from the grave. God gave Jesus Christ the power to conquer and defeat death. What greater love is there? There isn't!

He has literally done what no one else has ever done. Someone reading this may say, well He died for me, I would die for someone I love! Hey, I agree with you! I would die for someone I love too, but would you die for the entire world even though they didn't deserve it? Would you die for those who don't know you, those who don't like you and those who persecute you, like your enemies for instance? No, you wouldn't! It doesn't even make sense to do such a thing, but He loved us so much that He died for all of us. Even though God loves us, He cannot endure sin. I remember I wanted a clearer understanding on this, so I prayed about it then God spoke to me.

One day I was driving in my car on my way to pick my husband up from work and I said, "Father why is it that the world doesn't know you and why is it that some can't hear from you directly?" He replied and said, "I can't tolerate sin, it stinks in my nostrils." Then He allowed a horrible odor, like a raw, stink, fishlike smell to blow into my car. Now mind you all of my windows were closed while driving. Immediately, I begin to praise God and thank Him for that revelation.

Even though I felt as though I couldn't endure the smell, I understood what He demonstrated. For God to be around any form of sinful nature, it would literally contradict His entire being. It's very important to turn from our sinful ways, so that we can have a closer relationship with God.

When we turn from sin, we are more prone to hear from God. There are so many things that God wants to reveal to us, but if our lives don't line up with His will, it will be very difficult to hear from Him directly.

For example, I'm not saying it's a sin to watch television, however too much of it can hinder you from hearing from God, especially if it doesn't give Him any glory. The same goes with music or anything else for that matter. If you want to hear from God directly, it is important to remove anything that is unclean in your life.

When we're out of the will of God, we're also out of the covering of God and I don't know about you, but I want to be in His covering. I want to be surrounded by His love, grace and mercy. I want to have the same relationship with God as Abraham, Moses and Peter did. I don't want to depend on others to give me a word from heaven and I definitely don't want to wait to hear it preached on Sunday mornings either. Instead I want to hear from God directly so that when I go to church, it's nothing but confirmation.

The number one way to hear from God directly is to put yourself in position. You can hear from Him when you read your Bible daily, seek after Him daily and live a prayer-filled life. Then will God reveal Himself to you.

WHAT MUST I DO TO BE SAVED?

Acts 16:31 tells us that if we believe in the Lord Jesus Christ, we shall be saved. Romans 10:9 tells us that if anyone calls on the name of Jesus they shall be saved. If you haven't received Jesus Christ as your personal savior, then you haven't received the gift of eternal life. If you want to be free from the bondages of sin, then give your heart to Jesus right now. You cannot afford to put this off.

Time is winding down and Jesus is coming soon. Many people don't give their lives to God because they feel as though what they've done in their life is just too bad and God couldn't possibly forgive them, but that's not true. That is a trick of the adversary and he's been using this scheme since the beginning of time. Many people are lost forever all because they believed that God couldn't forgive someone like them. Listen, when Jesus died on that cross, He knew exactly what He was dying for.

He died for the stripper, the murderer, the adulterer, the unbeliever and His enemies too, which are people who don't believe in Him at all.

He died for every sin which means that He died for all of us because we were all born a sinner and it's very important to know that. Don't ever feel like God could never forgive you because of something terrible you may have done.

Often times while doing street ministry, I would come across people who flat out feel as though they did the worst thing ever and God could never forgive them of their sins. Others sometimes believe that Jesus didn't die for such a sin as theirs. This hurts me to my heart because I know that the devil fed them those lies. Jesus died for every sin and Jesus loves all of us, no matter what we've done in our lives. God is a forgiver and His love endures forever. No matter what you have done, I repeat, no matter what you have done, God will forgive you, but you must give your life to Him, repent with a sincere heart and turn from your sins.

Tomorrow isn't promised to us which means that if you have not given your life to Jesus Christ and repented for all your sins, you would be forever lost, out of the presence of God and forever in torment. Now God knows that you are not perfect, but all He wants is your heart. Scripture tells us that if we love Him, we will keep his commandments.

Then Peter said unto them, Repent, and be baptized every one of you in the name of Jesus Christ for the remission of sins, and ye shall receive the gift of the Holy Ghost.
-Acts 2:38

Also while ministering, people would tell me that they're too deep in sin and they feel that there's absolutely no way out. They feel that when the time is right, they will get saved. However, there is never a right time other than right now.

If you are reading this book, then the time is now. Don't wait until tomorrow to get saved. Tomorrow isn't promised to us, which means tomorrow could be too late. Give your life to Jesus right now, He has been waiting for you!

The only thing that sin has to offer you is eternal torment. I told you from the beginning that your salvation was important to me. I just want to make sure that you receive the gift that Jesus has for you. You must understand that the devil doesn't want you to know that there's an option for salvation. He just wants you to think that you are born to live and live to die. He doesn't want you to prepare for the afterlife.

Remember, God loves you and will accept you just the way you are. In the Bible, Saul was really far from God. He didn't believe in Jesus at all. In fact, he was a persecutor of anyone who did, but one day on his way to Damascus, Jesus appeared to him, blinded him and when Saul realized that Jesus was really the Messiah, he was on fire for the Lord and served Him ever since

Once you accept Jesus Christ as your Lord and personal savior, Paul then refers to you as the body of Christ because you are no longer living for this corrupt world, but you are to live your life holy for God. Paul also says that we must not be transformed by the world, but by the renewing of our mind. This means that you must make up in your mind that you are going to live for God and for God alone.

If you want to be free of sin, delivered from bondage, and have eternal life with the

Father, then let Him in your heart. He will change your life around. God wants to be a part of your everyday life, so just let Him in. He loves you.

5 STEPS TO SALVATION

1st.   You must acknowledge that you are a sinner.

For all have sinned, and come short of the glory of God.
-Romans 3:23

2nd.   You must believe that Jesus is the son of God and that He died for your sins and rose on the third day.

He that believeth on the Son hath everlasting life: and he that believeth not the Son shall not see life; but the wrath of God abideth on him.
-John 3:36

3rd.   Ask God to forgive you of all your sins.

If we confess our sins, he is faithful and just to forgive us our sins, and to cleanse us from all unrighteousness.
-1 John 1:9

4th.   Accept Jesus as your Lord and Savior.

Jesus saith unto him, I am the way, the truth, and the life: no man cometh unto the Father, but by me.
-John 14:6

5th. Confess Jesus as your Lord and Savior and be filled with the Holy Ghost.

In whom ye also trusted, after that ye heard the word of truth, the gospel of your salvation: in whom also after that ye believed, ye were sealed with that Holy Spirit of promise.
-Ephesians 1:13

If you truly believe what you've just read, then say this prayer with a sincere heart and God will forgive you of all your sins.

Dear Jesus, please forgive me for all of my sins. I believe that you are the Son of God and you shed your precious blood for me. Your word says that if I confess that you are Lord and believe that God raised you from the dead, then I shall be saved. So right now, I confess that you are my Lord and Savior and I believe that you conquered the grave when you died and rose from the dead. Now according to your Word, I am saved. So Lord I ask that you transform my life, teach me how to live holy and acceptable to you and create in me a clean heart in Jesus name I pray, amen.

Congratulations!!! If you said this prayer with a sincere heart, then God has heard your cry and Jesus is now your Lord and personal Savior. Now that you have accepted Jesus Christ into your heart, you have accepted the gift of eternal life.

I want to encourage you to find a local church home and get baptized. Jesus Christ now lives inside of you and you are now promised everlasting life. Heaven is now rejoicing because you have repented and turned away from sin.

THE TRUTH SHALL SET YOU FREE!

This is the part where I tell you that just because you gave your life to God doesn't mean that your life is going to be peachy cream from this point on. Listen, I would be so wrong if I didn't tell you the truth.

Now that you are a believer, you will face many obstacles in life especially temptations. You will also go through many storms, trials and tribulations, but it's very important to know that God will be with you every step of the way. If you are tempted and you end up sinning, immediately repent with a sincere heart and refrain from committing that sin again.

THE WORD OF GOD STRENGTHENS YOU

The Word of God tells us that a righteous man's steps are ordered by God. This simply means that as long as you live holy and acceptable unto the Lord and have the desire to obey Him, He will honor your prayers, provide all of your needs, and protect you from the plans of the adversary. You now have a covenant with the Father and a covering of protection over your life.

Now can I be real with you? I really want to keep it one hundred right now. Temptations come in many different shapes, sizes and colors. Have you ever told yourself that you knew something wasn't good for you, but yet it seems like no matter how hard you try, somehow you always give in? Rather it be cursing, drugs, lying or fornication, etc.

It's because you've been trying to overcome these temptations by yourself. By using this strategy, you are more likely to fail. If you depend on your own strength to overcome temptations, then you are fooling yourself, because our flesh desires the sin of this world.

The only way to overcome temptation is to establish a relationship with God. Also, by reading your Bible everyday will give you the strength you need to endure and overcome any obstacles that may come your way. Always remember that the word of God strengthens us!

I'm going to share with you a secret that has been working for me and many other believers as well. The secret is that not everyone can just read the Bible and expect to get a full revelation of it. This example is proven when the Religious leaders would read the scrolls thinking that they were in the will of God, yet in reality they were so far from God, it wasn't even funny. Jesus refers to them as hypocrites.

You don't want to be one of the ones who feel that just because they read the Bible they are in the will of God. This is another trick of the adversary and it's sad that Satan is setting a lot of people up due to ignorance.

But the natural man receiveth not the things of the Spirit of God: for they are foolishness unto him: neither can he know them, because they are spiritually discerned.
-1 Corinthians 2:14

The only way to fully receive a divine revelation from God, you must be a believer, read your Bible and live a holy lifestyle. Then the word of God will give you the strength you need to overcome obstacles in your daily life. You still may be asking yourself, "How is this so?" Well what happens is, when a believer is living according to the Bible and is seeking God for an answer, deliverance, direction or clarity, etc., our spirit-man literally becomes hungry for God.

The hungrier we are for God, the more the Holy Spirit feeds us the Word of God. And in return will keep us from given into temptation and committing any sin.

You must know that you are very important to the body of Christ. With that being said, join a church home, fellowship and most importantly get involved. Being around other believers who are striving for righteousness will also give you strength, but please note, this journey in Christ for the most part can be a lonely road. Always remember, whatever you go through in life, you're not in it alone. Jesus will be right there with you every step of the way.

No matter the trials or tribulations, reach out to your brothers and sisters in Christ as they lift your situation in prayer. Having other believers intercede on your behalf helps you to fight, stand strong and encourages you to grow spiritually.

I am full of excitement just knowing that another soul is now saved and set free from the bondages of sin. I personally want to welcome you to the body of Christ. Congratulations!!! You are now promised everlasting life!

CHAPTER 2

I'm Saved! Now What?

Now that you are a believer, one of the first steps to growing in your walk with Christ is to read your bible daily. This is the number one way you can actually connect with God personally. There are so many versions and translations out there, but I recommend you read from the, (KJV) King James Version.

Some people may find it very difficult to read, but what you don't understand, you can always ask the Holy Spirit to give you a revelation. By doing so, this builds your relationship with God, to depend on Him for understanding. There is nothing like asking God a question and waiting for Him to respond and He does it.

Ask, and it shall be given you; seek, and ye shall find; knock, and it shall be opened unto you.
-Matthew 7:7

This is one of my favorite scriptures. I love it because it reminds me that the word of God is a living Word and the more I read it, the more knowledge I gain from it. The more you seek after God, the more you will find in Him, and anything you ask of Him, He will reveal unto you.

WHERE DO I BEGIN?

Many people don't know where to begin in their new journey with Christ. Let's be honest here. The minute you leave the altar after you have received Jesus as your Lord and savior, is the minute that you will need clear direction as to where to go from here. The best advice I have for you is to treat your relationship with God like a real relationship, just as you would with someone you really care about.

Jesus is your number one friend. You can call on Him anytime and He will answer. Anytime you're in doubt or in fear, just pray! He'll be there. Here are some tips towards a successful walk with Christ:

- Read your Bible daily.
- Live a prayerful life.
- Live a lifestyle of repentance.
- Resist the enemy and he will flee.
- Always seek after the Word of God.
- Always set a Godly example.

- Pray for covering over your mind.
- Pray for covering over your body.
- Pray for covering over your families, finances, transportation, health, etc.
- Seek to be available in ministry.
- Pray for others to be saved, set-free and delivered.

It is very important to read the bible for yourself. Don't go by what you've heard someone else say or what someone else believes. It is important to go by what the spirit of God reveals to you. Now it may be very challenging in the beginning hearing from God, but the more you read your Bible and seek after Him, He will reveal Himself to you more and more. Now if you haven't read the bible before or don't know where to begin, just pray first and ask God to lead you to a scripture to read. A lot of times just by praying first before reading, God sends us to the exact scripture we need. Most importantly, even if you have read the whole entire Bible before, there is still so much more to learn.

It is very important to read your bible every day. It doesn't matter if you read a verse, a chapter or an entire book a day. Just as long as you read it and abide by it, that's all that matters. Just like the old saying goes, "A little bit really does go a long way."

I love reading the Bible because it's a living Word and there's a scripture that I can apply to every aspect of my everyday life.

For example, when in doubt, I can refer to Mark 11:23. When in pain, I read Jeremiah 33:6 and when in fear, I can stand on 2 Timothy 1:7.

Now if you have a smart phone, there are many free Bible apps in the android market, but my favorite is Bible.is because it's such a handy source for your Bible studying needs. You can hear the word audibly while driving or sleeping, you can highlight or take notes, download scriptures to your phone, watch biblical movies, translate any Bible version to thousands of languages and so much more.

Like I said there are many other Bible apps, but I find this one to be the best. If you don't have a smart phone or access to the internet, you can always visit your local Christian book store and purchase the right Bible just for you.

LIVING A PRAYERFUL LIFE

As a child of God, it is very important to make up in your mind that you will dedicate a lifestyle of prayer. In Luke 18:1 it tells us that we must always pray and not faint and 1 Thessalonians 5:17 tells us that we must pray without ceasing. Now let's think about this for a minute. According to some research I've done on Google, I found out that on an average we may speak anywhere from 3,000 to 20,000 words a day and possibly more if you're someone who loves to talk or have a lot on your mind. Just as often as we open our mouths to talk to our colleagues, family members or friends, it is very important to open our mouths to pray daily. By doing so, this strengthens your prayer life as well as builds your relationship with God.

With additional research, I've also found out that on an average we may think anywhere from 50,000-70,000 thoughts per day which is an average of 30-40 thoughts per minute. With that being said, out of all those thoughts, how many of these thoughts are on our kids, our jobs, ourselves, or the things we do or need to do? Now how many of these thoughts are on the Lord? How many of these thoughts are on worshiping God? How many of these thoughts are on you giving Him praise, and what thoughts are you having on pleasing Him? You must understand that by keeping your mind stayed on the Lord, keeps you in the will of God.

Have you ever taken a moment to process your thoughts? Without processing your thoughts, your mind can end up terribly unbalanced. You must note that every thought that enters your mind is not all yours.

Literally every time a thought enters into your mind, you must identify where it's coming from. Without processing your thoughts, if you're not careful, anything that comes to your mind, you may be capable of acting it out, simply because you would think it's just you thinking all of those terrible thoughts. But in reality, the devil will try to communicate to you through your mind too. How do you think he's able to tempt us without anyone else ever knowing? It starts in the mind and the devil knows that. I will touch more on this later, but right now I want to show you why it's so important to process your thoughts.

What happens is as we pray God may drop something in your spirit, but if you're not careful you may not know where it's coming from. The enemy is very conniving and loves to portray God, when in reality he's nothing but a counterfeit. He could never be the real deal, but God assures us not to worry because he says that his sheep which is you and I knows his voice. So the more we have a prayer-filled lifestyle, the more we will understand when God's talking to us, wanting to show us something, or trying to give us a clear direction.

This is why we must have our minds stayed on God at all times. Even though it may seem impossible, trust me it's possible. Communication with God through prayer is everything. Your prayers will build your faith in knowing that God will reveal, God will answer and God will confirm. Your prayers will help you to be sensitive to the Spirit of God.

HEARING FROM GOD

One of the first things you must understand is that God does not want religion from you, only a relationship. It's so easy to get caught up in tradition or religion and that's the complete opposite of what God wants. All God want's is you! You are a child of God now and you must know who you are.

But ye are a chosen generation, a royal priesthood, a holy nation, a peculiar people; that ye should shew forth the praises of him who hath called you out of darkness into his marvelous light;

-1 Peter 2:9

There were many times in my life when I felt as though I was distant from God. I've been saved for as long as I can remember, but it was very difficult to hear from the Lord. Yes I was saved, but I didn't understand my purpose. I'd go to church and everything and yes, the preaching was good, but I always desired to hear a word just for me. I wanted God to speak to me personally. Now even though I had this desire, it seemed as though many times I would leave the exact same way I came. Rather it be because of bitterness, not growing spiritually or walking in extreme disobedience.

I've come to the realization that the Father wasn't distant from me, but I from Him. Ever since then I've learned that it's important to seek after the Lord whole heartedly, because the more we seek after Him, the more He reveals. I've learned that I was putting other things before God like time for instance. I had to learn to stop putting other things before God and allow Him to be first in my everyday life and this included everything.

As children of God we must be in a position to hear from God. He's always speaking, but the question is, are we listening? Ever since I've changed my way of thinking, my way of living began to change also.

Now I often find myself not being able to go on about my day unless I've heard from the Lord. If I haven't heard from God then I would literally feel like a lost sheep who wandered too far from its shepherd and that's not a good feeling.

Now my relationship has grown significantly with the Lord. I've made it a habit to pray several times a day before I rise and before I lay down. I also set aside times periodically throughout the day to read my bible and pray. By doing so, this helps me to hear clearly from God. This puts me in the right position to hear from the Lord.

A lot of times it isn't always a formal setting when I go before the Lord. Many times I go before my Father's presence in my secret closet and one thing I love about my secret closet is that it's relocatable. It's not always the perfect setting of me laying prostrate before the altar, with a prayer shawl over my head, anointing my forehead while taking communion.

Often times, my prayer closet is while I'm driving down the road or lying in my bed, studying my Bible and before I fall asleep, I would pray again and receive revelation of what I just read. There's been so many times, I would fall asleep after reading my Bible and God would begin to reveal unto me many things. So you see? That's one of His ways of speaking.

Other times when I'm relaxed in my bed while reading the Bible, I'd get a revelation from God through visions right before I nod off to sleep. It's always exciting for me to receive a dream or vision from God.

I believe that if you enhance your prayer life, you will begin to receive revelation from the Father as well.

LIVE IN HUMILITY NOT FEAR!

One night, I had just finished reading my Bible and fell asleep. During my sleep, I had a dream of a brown female bear who somehow wandered onto my street where I live. I was outside my house, but when I saw her my first instinct was to run inside due to fear. However, I instantly became very concerned for the bear, because she looked hungry. So I lured her towards me with some food and she followed behind me as I invited her into my house.

Even though the bear was very intimidating due to her size and her growl, she was very friendly and bonded with all of us immediately.

There were several occasions in my dream when her and I would wrestle as we were playing, but eventually I had to place her in my garage, so that she could have more room to maneuver. I eventually thought to myself,

"Man if she's this friendly, she could live with us and I could take care of her."

When I woke up from that dream, I said, "God, please explain to me why I had this silly dream." Immediately, the Lord dropped in my spirit, "Don't live in fear, live in humility!" This dream reminded me of another dream I had a little over a year ago.

In this dream there was a lioness coming from a wooded area across the street from my house. I was so fascinated by seeing this beautiful beast in my neighborhood so I invited her into my house. When she came in, I could tell that she was very tired, hungry and thirsty, so I gave her some water to drink.

All of my children in the house loved her and she began to bond with all of us immediately. At first she was very friendly, then she quickly became aggressive and began to growl at us. I knew I had to feed her quickly or else we would all be done for.

So I quickly grabbed some lunch meat out of the refrigerator and then she calmed down while she was eating. After she ate, she began to play with the children again and she stayed at the house a little while longer until I could tell that something was bothering her. I assumed she was ready to leave. I then opened the side door of my garage, which led her outside and she eventually went on her way.

Now, I questioned God about this, because I still didn't understand why I had this dream and why He brought the other one to my remembrance. Well this is what I got from the dream. For starters, lioness' are hunters. When they're away from their den, they're most likely looking for prey to bring back to feed their cubs. However, when I saw her, my first instincts were that I wasn't afraid.

A few hours later, I woke up because I had to get my youngest son ready for school. So I quickly got him and my daughter dressed, fed them and we rushed out of the house.

I didn't have a car at the time, but being that the school was only a few blocks away, I would always walk him to school while pushing my youngest daughter in a stroller.

This particular day, we were about half way to the school, when all of a sudden there was a pit bull across the street, barking aggressively.

Now I'm no animal whisperer, however, I knew that dog was ready to attack. I quickly began to pray, because I knew that my children and I were in great danger.

Fear quickly gripped my heart and right away, I felt very helpless. Then I asked God for wisdom and immediately, He dropped down in my spirit to invite the dog over towards us. So I began to talk very sweetly to him and I whistled at him to get his attention. I got down real low to balance myself on my knees, so that he could see that I was not afraid and that I posed no threat to him either. I reached out my arms towards him and said, "Come here baby, come here boy!" As sweetly as I possibly could.

Then the funniest thing happened. Well, it wasn't funny then, but it sure is funny now. If only you could have seen the look on his face. He looked very confused and I could tell that the dog was really thinking about his next move. He then looked one way, then looked the other. Then he sat in a doglike position and thought about it some more. About thirty seconds later, he continued on about his way in the opposite direction.

I continued to pray while walking my son to school, because I wanted a revelation from the Lord. I couldn't believe what happened and why the dog didn't attack us like he intended to. Then God dropped in my spirit, "Living in humility removes all fear!" He showed me that if I live humble before Him, I have nothing to fear.

That just blessed me and to add on to that, just by living by this very concept literally it saved our lives. I honestly believe that the dream I had earlier that day, was God preparing me to be humble in the situation that later took place. God began to deal with me more on this matter and this is what I learned. When we live in humility and not fear, you can then sit back and watch the peace of God consume your everyday situations.

WHAT IS MY PURPOSE?

I can assure you that if you have been through something very tragic in your life, not only will God bring you out of it, but He wants to use that situation as a major significance in your ministry.

Someone may be asking, "How did I end up homeless?" Or, "Why did I have to go through that when I was younger, etc.?" Well I feel led to tell you that no matter what you've been through in life, the good, the bad or the extreme ugly, God still has a purpose and a plan for your life!

Sure you may not understand why you had to go through it, but God knows the ultimate reason why and if you are obedient and harken to His voice no matter what you've been through or what you are currently going through, He will bring you out of it!

God does not want you to be upset with Him for allowing you to go through it, He wants you to trust in Him that He will bring you out of it!

Do you remember the story of Job in the Bible? God allowed Satan to try Job in every way possible. He ended up with a terrible disease and the devil stole everything from him. Even his children died in the midst of his most trying times, but he did not lose his faith in God. His faith was unshakable! He trusted in God no matter what and in the end, God restored everything. It was literally, doubled for his trouble.

Now you may be asking yourself, "My ministry?" Yes, I didn't stutter when I said it, "Your Ministry!" Whatever you have been through or are currently going through, God still wants to use you for His glory. He wants to use you to comfort and be a blessing to others who've been through the exact same thing!

I'm sure you've heard that old saying, "Everything happens for a reason!" Well, let me tell you, that is so true! Even though a lot of things we go through are caused by the choices we make in life, there are still so many things that happens to us that are literally out of our control.

Let's look at a scenario of a child who has been sexually abused by their father. Even though everyone's story is different, the stories I mostly hear about are ones which are similar to this. Now I'm just using this as an example here. However, I've been in many confidential conversations where this was the case.

The title of this scenario is: *"No Matter What You're Going Through, God Can Bring You Out of It!"* Now before I go more into this scenario, there are a couple of things that I want to point out here.

1. Spirits do travel.
2. Generational curses are real.
3. And we wrestle with real demonic forces every single day.

In this scenario, the child chooses to be a bisexual, homosexual, etc., because of what was done to them by their father, but what the child doesn't know is that their grandfather or great uncle sexually abused their father when he was younger. Now if the child's father would have lived a consecrated lifestyle and trusted in the Lord just as Job did, God would have not only saved him, but delivered and set him free from all demonic forces.

I want to also point out that if the father would have taken his childhood situation before the Lord, lived a consecrated lifestyle and trusted in the Lord, God would have also used him to comfort and be a blessing to others, including his child and this scenario would have had a different outcome.

This scenario would have gone something like: There was a man who had a child and even though he was sexually abused when he was younger, instead of allowing these spirits to travel through generational curses, he is now an amazing, powerful and anointed man of God who is living a holy-filled lifestyle and people such as his child and others who know him look up to him, as he looks up to God. Because even though what he went through was very tragic and unfortunate, he brought his problems before the Lord and God delivered him and used him in a mighty way.

The problem today is that many people are faced with situations similar to this and don't understand why they had to go through it. Have you realized that a lot of times, it's the ones who have a calling on their lives that go through the most trials and tribulations? It's time to ask yourself why.

So when I say your ministry, that's exactly what I mean. Listen, my story may not be the same as yours or the next person, but one thing is for sure, God loves you and He has a purpose and a plan for your life, no matter what you've been through.

Don't ever feel like because of your past, God can't use you! Even if it was your fault, God is a forgiver of every sin. The only thing God wants from you is a sincere heart. Remember God wants to use what you been through for His glory.

Have you ever asked these questions? "What is my purpose for living or why am I here?" I know I have. Once we accept Jesus Christ as our Lord and savior, Paul then refers to us as the body of Christ. This means that we are no longer living for the world, but living our lives for God. This doesn't mean that we won't go through anything, because we will go through many things, but if we stand on the Word of God and His promises, He will guide us through it all.

THE RENEWING OF YOUR MIND

So many people find themselves struggling really bad naturally, physically and emotionally because they are caught up in the things of this world.

In cases such as these, what's actually taking place is, they're focusing more on their problems rather than trusting that God can bring them out of it.

When God created man, He created us in such a phenomenal way to depend solely on Him, so that He can provide for all of our needs. Even down to the air we breathe, which is literally the breath of God. The problem is, many people are losing focus and don't understand their purpose for living.

Paul says, "Do not be transformed by the world, but by the renewing of your mind." This is why it is so important to get our minds right.

Our minds must always dwell on the Lord. If our minds are kept on the cares of the world then we are not living according to the will of God, because God doesn't want us living in worry, fear, regret, etc.

Therefore, be sure to keep your mind stayed on the Lord and dedicate yourself in worship and prayer and your relationship will grow stronger in Him.

CHAPTER 3

Delivered from Darkness

When Jesus gave His life for us, He died for every last one of our sins. He sacrificed His life so that we can be free from the hands of the enemy, but keep in mind that we'll still face many trials and tribulations. Have you ever questioned why so many believers are struggling in their everyday lives or why most Christians struggle with situations that seems to hinder them from growing spiritually? In this chapter, I will teach you how to be delivered and set free from anything that's hindering you to grow in your relationship with God.

WHAT'S HINDERING YOU?

When it comes to the bondages of the enemy, the list goes on and sadly to say, there's so many people who feel as though they can't let go of their sins and this is where they give the enemy authority over their lives. In other words, when we're out of the will of God, we're literally giving the devil permission to bring problems upon us. Now don't get me wrong, we're all going to face many obstacles, trials and tribulations in life, but if we stand on the Word of God, our Father in heaven will carry us through it all.

Ask yourself these questions, what are somethings that are hindering me from moving forward in life? What are somethings that are hindering me from growing in my relationship with God?

I have included a few common reasons why many believers find it very difficult to grow spiritually. Before checking to see if any of these hindrances apply to you, ask God to reveal your struggles and pay close attention to anything you may battle with.

- Depression
- Disobedience
- Anger
- Un-forgiveness
- Bitterness
- Lust
- Adultery
- Fornication
- Drugs
- Masturbation
- Pornography
- Lying
- Stealing
- Manipulation
- Unclean Desires/Fantasies
- Poor Health

- Poor Faith
- Etc.

Do you struggle with any of these obstacles? Believe it or not, many people do, especially within the body of Christ. If you want to be free from all bondages of sin then pray to God with a sincere heart. Ask Him to forgive you and He will purify your soul.

There were many times in life when I struggled with hindrances that kept me out of the will of God, but one day I made avowal to Him that I will not partake of anything that doesn't line up with His will and I've kept my covenant with Him ever since.

In my early teens I was saved, yet I was struggling in my walk with Christ. Just to mention a few of my problems, I struggled with lying, cursing, stealing, lust, fornication and even masturbation. The world would look at this as a normal way of living, but I knew I wasn't living according to the will of God.

Now there was a time during my struggles when I really wanted to change my ways, but it became harder and harder for me and I didn't fully know how to overcome them.

I didn't realize that I was leaning on my own understanding, (my own strength) and not the Word of God. This is where the spirit of depression and suicide snuck in. I got to a point where I no longer wanted to live, because I knew that I wasn't perfect. I knew I was unworthy and I knew that God was not pleased. I knew I was a hypocrite living a double life and I began to feel like there was no purpose for me to live.

Even though these obstacles would bring me temporary satisfaction, I was still miserable and I wanted a change. These hindrances had me so deep in sin. I was saved, yet I wasn't delivered. As a result, I was on my way to hell.

The purpose of me sharing this with you is, because this is my testimony. No one really knew what I was going through, but all because I had a sincere heart to change my wicked ways, the Lord kept me and delivered me.

So now, not only am I saved, I am also set free and filled with the Holy Ghost. I have literally figured out how to overcome any attacks of the enemy and that's simply by standing on the Word of God.

HOW TO OVERCOME BACKSLIDING

God is not pleased with anyone who lives a double life. Even being lukewarm in this walk is very dangerous. Some people make up their minds to get on the right track and they would literally go to church on Sunday, give their praises to God and repent for all of their sins, yet from a Monday through a Saturday they would live without any Biblical standards.

Living this kind of lifestyle is literally like playing with fire. Always remember, to overcome the struggles of back-sliding, you must completely turn from sin.

The devil is not going to stop trying you just because you may be too week to fight. John 10:10 says that the enemy comes to steal, kill and to destroy us.

This means that because you are a child of God, the devil will not stop until you fall. So even though he comes with all of his fiery darts, it does not mean that you have to yield to any temptation or fear. God has given you all the power you need to overcome anything the devil throws your way.

Now there are many weapons to overcome all trials, tribulations and even the temptations of the world. As a result of using them, you will have the power needed to overcome all obstacles in life.

The number one weapon is the Word of God, which is the Sword of the Spirit. This means that if you apply it to your everyday life along with fasting and praying, it will give you the strength you need to overcome and it will also help you to fight effectively.

Here are some other weapons to help you overcome the struggle of backsliding.

The Weapon of Love

Have you ever heard the saying, "Love Conquers All"? Well it's true. God says, "If you love me, you will keep my commandments."

Now I can't speak for everyone, but I love Him and I desire to please Him in every way. Having this kind of mindset will keep you in a state of worship.

Because He has always provided every last one of my needs, shown me unconditional love and continues to show me grace, mercy and unusual favor, I love Him for that and I give Him my life.

The Weapon of Prayer

Did you know that prayer is a powerful weapon? Every time you pray, you tap into a spiritual realm and God gives you the authority to operate in it. Literally, with enough power you can command demons to flee.

In 1 Thessalonians 5:17, Paul instructs us to pray without ceasing. This means that we must always be in prayer. The reason is because of the warfare that takes place spiritually. Even though we can't see what's going on through our carnal eyes, with faith, we can tear down the principalities of any demonic force that rises up against us.

Now if our minds are stayed on God and constantly praying against the plans of the enemy, then we have already overcome. Always keep in mind that our adversary does not want us to know how powerful we are when we live a prayer-filled life.

Have you ever noticed that every time you try to walk in the will of God, it seems like immediately you are faced with a situation that wasn't a problem before or something that was an issue from your past is a problem again? It's because the devil is attacking you spiritually. His plans are to get you off track in your walk with Christ and he can achieve that by destroying your faith.

He doesn't want you to know that every time you pray, you are tossing him a few blows right in the face and every time you overcome him, you send demonic forces back defeated.

Be sure to keep in mind that any and everything that rises up against you is spiritual warfare and now you know the key elements to fight effectively in it.

The Weapon of an Open Confession

James 5:16 tells us to confess our sins one to another. By doing so, you will have the power and strength to overcome what's hindering you. Remember the saying, "What's done in the dark, stays in the dark?" Well that's true, until it's exposed by light and that light is the Word of God.

The devil knows that if your sins are kept a secret, he has some authority over you. So no matter what that "something" may be, openly confess your faults! Even if it's uncomfortable to talk about, confess! It doesn't matter what people think of you, the important thing is you being free from whatever is keeping you in sin.

The Weapon of Worship

Worship is not only a sacrifice, but also a weapon. In a literal sense, it's intimacy with God. The more intimate you are with Him, the more your relationship deepens and the stronger you will be in Him. This will give you a firmer foundation and your faith will be unshakable.

Many people may not understand my worship, but it doesn't matter. God accepts every bit of it, because it's sincere. I want to encourage you to live a lifestyle of worship. In doing so, will establish a beautiful, long lasting relationship with the Godhead.

THE POWER OF LOVE

On several accounts, I've personally been asked, "How can someone be free from sin and overcome the temptations of darkness completely?" My response is always this, "If you love God and desire to please Him then everything else will fall in place." In other words, your desire for sin will disappear, because you have a passion to please God, but if you love and desire the things of the world then that's grounds for a struggling walk.

If you love God then a drive for obedience will kick in. A hunger and thirst for the Lord will soon follow. Love is the key element that keeps you from falling into sin.

With love, God will give you the power to overcome all things. I believe God is going to do something great and miraculous in your life. How do I know this? Because of the unconditional love that he has for you. You just keep on seeking the face of God and stand on His Word and He will literally move mountains for you!

I always say, if my mind is stayed on the Lord then I can't go wrong. Why? Because I'm in the will of God, I'm in the right position to hear from Him and I have a desire to please Him as well. All I want is for God to be proud of me and all He wants is for me to love Him unconditionally. When we love God, living holy then becomes easy.

THE POWER OF PRAYER

One day I heard the spirit of the Lord say, "Just because God hasn't answered yet, doesn't mean He's forgotten about you." Then immediately the Lord gave me a revelation.

In the Bible, Martha told Jesus if you had been here, Lazarus would still be alive, yet Jesus still showed up and raised him from the dead.

I want to encourage you that God hasn't forgotten about you. He has heard every prayer and will answer right on time. So continue to:

- Walk in faith
- Go to God in prayer
- Stand on His promises

THE POWER OF AN OPEN CONFESSION

Have you ever asked God to forgive you for a particular sin, yet somehow you kept falling back into it over and over again? If so, then it's time out for playing around with God. If you're serious about getting delivered and set free then it's time to go to God with a sincere heart, asking Him to forgive you. It would also be wise to have a man or woman of God cover you in prayer concerning your faults. The purpose of this is not to confess your sins to them, but for them to continually intercede for your deliverance.

Here's a quick testimony of what I mean. Many years ago, I went to a church service where the pastor preached a moving sermon. During the altar call, he mentioned that if anyone wanted to be set free from sin, there was no longer a need for any circumstances to be kept in secret. He said that now was the time to expose the enemy and be set free.

He asked all the men intercessors to quickly form a few prayer circles for the men who needed deliverance and asked every woman intercessor to do the same. Then he asked everyone who wanted to be delivered and set free to go to any group they chose to confess their sins.

Immediately, all of the intercessors stood in the gap and prayed against all demonic forces that were hindering the people and the power of God broke many chains in that place.

I was so moved, that I ended up in one of the group circles. I then began to openly confess my struggling sins before the Lord. Now let me tell you, at first I was really embarrassed and I almost didn't confess at all, but I knew I wanted to be set free. So I cried out and said, "Lord I want to be delivered and I know only you can do it! I no longer want anything to do with masturbation anymore. Please deliver me from anything that's not like you!" Then the intercessors prayed for me and immediately I was set free.

Now am I saying that I never had those temptations ever again? Of course I did. In fact, it got worst, but because I stood on the Word of God, and my prayer warriors had my back, I was able to overcome all demonic forces.

WORSHIP IS MY WEAPON

As for me, when it comes to spiritual warfare, I find that worshipping God gives me strength. During worship, I'm reminded of His unconditional love, mercy and favor and because of His unconditional love alone, He is worthy of all my praise and worship.

Because worship is another form of an offering, I want to be found giving my best at all times. For instance, when I wake up in the morning and get that good stretch in, I'm also giving God a wave offering, because He didn't have to wake me up.

OVERCOMING TEMPTATION

In my late teens, I was a member of Abundant Life located in Jacksonville, FL where Pastor Derrick Cole was and still is the pastor of that church. One day, he said to the congregation, "Stop trying not to sin and try to live holy!"

Let me tell you, I am now in my early thirties and I'm still standing on that same principle. I plan on keeping this mindset until the Lord calls me home or when Jesus returns. Why? Because it actually works.

Listen, I know how hard it is to walk away from sin. I remember every day, I would start my day out saying, "Today, I'm not going to lie." "Today, I'm not going to lust!" See the problem was, I was making promises to myself instead of asking God to keep me. As a result, I gave into temptation every single time.

It wasn't until I sought the face of God. Literally, every single day I would ask Him for strength to overcome all sin and because I depended on Him, He's kept me all the way.

Here's another nugget to help you fight spiritually. Find yourself an accountability partner, someone who you know is seeking the face of God.

I have a friend who holds me accountable for everything I do and vise-versa. Why? Because we're spirit in the flesh and we need to always be sure that our lives line up with the Word of God. So if one of us are out of place then we'd have each other for encouragement and intercession.

There are no secrets in the kingdom of God anyway, so why are so many people keeping their struggling sin in the dark? Something to think about huh? It's because their too ashamed, embarrassed or don't want anyone to know their business? Please, it's not worth going to hell for.

It's time to stop hiding our struggling sins and it's time to expose the devil and be set free.

JESUS DIED FOR ME

I remember the first time I experienced the presence of God. I'll never forget because of the compassion I felt when the preacher was telling the congregation how Jesus died for our sins. After hearing those words confirming that I was a sinner and on my way to hell, I knew it should have been me. I was so touched that someone would do such a thing, all because they love me. So I began to cry right there in the middle of service. I remember my mom asking me what was wrong and I told her with tears rolling down my face that I was touched that Jesus died for me. I knew at that very moment, the least I could do was live my life for Him. During the altar call, my mom rushed me to the front of the church to get prayer and that was the very moment I was saved, set free, delivered and filled with the Holy Ghost. I was only six years old when I confessed Jesus Christ to be my Lord and Savior and my life has changed ever since.

Have you ever heard of the term "A baby Christian or a babe in Christ?" This term is used when a new believer is born again because they have received Jesus Christ as their Lord and personal savior. When I gave my life to the Lord, I was only six years old. Now if that's not a baby Christian, then I don't know what is. Literally! I was just a baby, but one thing I want to point out here is the moment I gave my life to Christ, was the moment I was a threat to Satan's kingdom. It didn't matter my age, from that day forward I was spiritually attacked.

EXPOSING THE ENEMY

Did you know the minute you received Jesus Christ as your personal savior, you were delivered from everything that was hindering you spiritually? A lot of times when temptation comes, many people fall right back into the same situation that God has brought them from. This is because they were not strong enough to overcome, but God has given all of us the ultimate power to defeat the enemy and that power is the Word of God.

When a believer gets saved they assume that it's going to take time to be fully delivered, but according to 1 John 1:7, it tells us that if we walk in the light which is the Word of God, the blood of Jesus Christ will cleanse us from all sin. This scripture points out that we must live according to the Word of God to defeat the devil.

Have you ever experienced going to church and being moved by the spirit of God and during service you've said something like, "Lord, I am going to let go of everything that's not in your will for my life!" Then as soon as you left from church, you were faced with overwhelming circumstances or life changing decisions to make?

For instance, you may have felt like you couldn't live without a certain individual because you need them to survive, knowing that person isn't good for you. Or maybe you felt like you couldn't stop doing certain things, because it helps you feel better and it helps you to accomplish other things, even though you know that God will not be pleased.

I want to enlighten you on what's been taken place. You have just made a commitment to God and the devil didn't like it, so he did everything in his power to prevent you from following through on what you knew was right.

When you were living out of the will of God, the devil had no problem with you because you weren't a threat to him, but the minute you decided to live your life fully for God, that was the minute everything changed. All of a sudden, the devil was trying to convince you that changing your life for the good was such a bad idea. Remember, he will do whatever it takes to get you to fall. He will even give you so many beneficial reasons why not to live for God.

WHEN THE TEMPTER COMES

One thing for sure, it doesn't matter who you are or what you believe, everyone gets tempted. Even Jesus was tempted. That's why we must acknowledge who the tempter really is and why he comes. Scripture tells us that God doesn't tempt us, but it's the devil who is our adversary. He is the tempter. He literally plots on strategic ways to set us up to fail.

So many people are struggling with many things which are keeping them separated from God. Just because someone holds a great title, doesn't mean they're never tempted. Truth is, they're more likely to be faced with many temptations. As for me, I'm tempted every single day, but when temptation comes, I find myself saying, "It's not worth my anointing!"

SAVED, DELIVERED AND SET FREE!

Many people believe they're saved all because they received Jesus Christ as their personal savior. While that's partially true, if they're even considering making it into the kingdom of God, there's so much that's required. We can't just proclaim that we're a Christian, yet do whatever we please. We must also live according to the Word of God.

And if the righteous scarcely be saved, where shall the ungodly and the sinner appear?
                                                    -1 Peter 4:18

There's so much more to just being saved. So many people are compromising now a days and are rooted in false teachings, yet are still on their way to hell. It's literally going to take turning away from sin and living according the Word of God. It's going to take a new way of thinking. That's why we must literally take on the mind of Christ and live according to the way He did. Now is the time to be saved, delivered and set free from all bondages of sin.

CHAPTER 4

A New Beginning

A few years ago, I held a discussion with a group of teenagers and I explained to them that every thought that goes through our mind are not always our own. They let me know they were relieved to hear that. Immediately, one of the teens mentioned that they were saved, yet they have thoughts on a daily basis that makes them feel like they're such a terrible person. I explained to them that we need to be very careful and pay more attention to our thoughts, because the devil likes to target our minds.

Therefore, if anyone is in Christ, he is a new creation. The old has passed away; behold, the new has come.

-2 Corinthians 5:17

Always remember, if our minds are not in the right place, it can be very difficult to get to where God is calling us. If the devil can get through to your mind then he can get through to you. Have you ever heard the old saying, "An idle mind is the devil's workshop?" Well that's not an actual scripture. However, there's still truth to that statement. If we keep our minds on God then our minds are in the right place.

Finally, brethren, whatsoever things are true, whatsoever things are honest, whatsoever things are just, whatsoever things are pure, whatsoever things are lovely, whatsoever things are of good report; if there be any virtue, and if there be any praise, think on these things.

-Philippians 4:8

After reading this scripture, you should be able to easily identify the enemy's thoughts. The simplest way to do this, is to see if it lines up with the Word of God. If it doesn't, then it came from Satan himself. Once you're able to identify Satan's thoughts, you don't have to sit there and entertain them. Scripture tells us that if we rebuke the devil, he has to flee.

Remember that search I did on Google? I wanted to see on an average, how many thoughts a person could have per day and to my surprise, my research was phenomenal. With an average person having up to 70,000 thoughts or more per day, I can't stress enough why it's so important to know where your thoughts are coming from.

PROCESSING YOUR THOUGHTS

In my younger years, I didn't always process my thoughts. As a matter of fact, I never knew I needed to. However, there were many times where one minute I would be at peace in my mind and the next I was all over the place with fear, anxiety or depression. Then there were times when I would have thoughts that would randomly cross my mind and ultimately encourage me to make sinful decisions, but one day, I got fed up and prayed about it. I asked the Lord to forgive me with a sincere heart and remove any desires that weren't His. I also let the devil know that I have a new mind and it's in Christ Jesus.

Ever since I prayed that prayer, God has equipped me with the power to overcome the devil. Now when temptation comes (especially in my mind), I'm able to recognize that it's Satan. The end result is, he gets rebuked and I have overcome him once again!

It wasn't until many years later that I realized the devil was having a field day in my mind, because he knew that if he could get to my mind then he could get to my heart. That's when I came up with a system called SMC (Simplified Mental Categories), and even till today, this strategy helps me to process my thoughts effectively.

Now I'm sure you're probably wondering how to process your own thoughts. Well it's simple. You must identify where every single thought is coming from. Based off of the title of my system, can you figure out how to break down your own thoughts into simplified categories? If not, that's okay. Listed below, I show you how the SMC system has helped me and I believe if you follow it, you'll be blessed as well.

UNDERSTANDING THE SMC SYSTEM

1st. Create a mental category for
"YOURSELF!"

By mentally creating this category in your mind leaves clarity in knowing that you are constantly thinking on the things you need to do or focus on today, tomorrow, or next year, etc. You may be studying for a test or you need to remember the items on your grocery list. Whatever your thoughts are, you would file them in this category.

2nd.   Create a mental category for
"SATAN!"

The devil is going to try whatever he can to tempt, hinder and even destroy you, but he cannot succeed unless you let him. Remember, he'll try to attack your mind first, but you can conquer every last plan by creating a category just for him. By doing so, you'll be able to recognize what he's up to. Now don't worry, I'm sure you're probably wondering how to know when thoughts are coming from the devil. Well, there's one important factor to stand on. The Bible says that he's the father of all lies. Therefore, if it doesn't line up with the Word of God then it's the devil. Be sure to be very prayerful during the processing of every thought, because the devil is also known to be a counterfeit. He loves to imitate the Father. So in the beginning, it can be very difficult to differentiate between every thought, but the more you continue to use this strategy, the easier it will be to defeat him.

3rd. *Create a mental category for* "GOD!"

Have you ever had a dream that you knew was spiritual and even though you didn't understand it, you knew there was a message behind it? Well that's one of Gods ways of speaking to you. I don't know how often you're having them, but there's so much that He wants to show you. He wants to talk with you directly through dreams, visions and even revelations. You can store all of His insights into this mental category. By doing so, will help you to block out all negativity and everything that's not of God. There will be many times when He will drop something in your spirit, so I also recommend that you keep a journal and jot down everything that comes from heaven especially promises. By creating this category, it will help you to be more sensitive to the voice of God.

4th.   Create a category for "UN-IDENTIFIED!"

This category is necessary especially if you're a newbie in Christ, because when you start out processing every thought, dream, vision, etc., it may be very difficult to know which ones are coming from God. If you're unsure of anything, just continue pray about it and God will give you clarity. Once you gain revelation, then you can mentally store the information in its proper category. As you grow spiritually, it will become easier to interpret and discern everything.

By implementing the SMC system along with praying, fasting and reading your Bible, not only will you be able to recognize the enemy, you will also gain understanding of God's voice more clearly. According to Ephesians 6:10-12, we live in a world that's not fully operated by flesh and blood, that's why we must recognize our adversary at all times.

WALKING IN YOUR CALLING

*"To walk in your calling
means to walk in extreme obedience."*

It may not look like it now, but there's purpose for your life. If you woke up this morning, then there's still an assignment that you need to fulfill. You may have always believed that there was a calling upon your life, but maybe you don't know where to begin. I want to encourage you to be sensitive to God. In other words, be obedient to Him, because if you have the desire to please Him, then walking in your calling will only come naturally.

Your calling will more than likely fall within your passion. For example, if you love to sing and teach, your calling could be to pursue a vocal coaching career, to sing professionally, or to draw others into praise and worship, etc. No matter what your calling is, the most important thing is to be available for God. Do you know what you're calling is? If not, continue to seek God and He will reveal it to you. As long as you're obedient to Him, He will lead and guide you into your divine purpose for living.

For I know the thoughts that I think toward you, saith the Lord, thoughts of peace, and not of evil, to give you an expected end.

-Jeremiah 29:11

There's been so many times when God has revealed a calling to someone, yet they don't answer the call. God may have shown them that they were called to preach or teach the gospel, but due to fear, disobedience or not trusting in Him, they decide not to do it.

For many are called, but few are chosen.
                                         -*Matthew 22:14*

IF GOD CALLED YOU TO IT THEN HE'S ANOINTED YOU TO DO IT

Listen, everyone is unique in their own way. However, many people get so jealous of others all because someone else may do something better. Instead of focusing on what others are doing, why not be found giving God your best?

To be called to do something, means that God has anointed you to do it. If you're not ready, then who do you suppose He use to get the job done right? It may just be your swag or personality that wins someone into the kingdom of God. Whatever you're called to do, remember, it's all about glorifying the Lord.

You may feel like you're not good enough, but Moses felt the exact same way. He told God that he couldn't speak to the people, because he had a stuttering problem, yet God still used him in a mighty way. If God has called you to do something, as long as you're willing, God will make a way.

Remember, God wants to use you and take you to a higher place spiritually, but it's going to take willingness and doing your best.

CONTINUE TO LOVE NO MATTER WHAT!

I recently had a dream that I was invited to speak at an all-white congregation. The church was in a small unrecognizable town, out in the country somewhere. After I preached the sermon, all the members showed us lots of love and invited us to come again soon. As we were preparing to leave, a few of the members invited us to a community banquet, they were attending later that evening. So we decided to stick around a little while longer to fellowship before heading back home.

While everyone was eating and having a nice time, I was approached by a tall white man, who had a stern look on his face. He was not pleased with us being there. I quickly discerned his spirit and God showed me that he had hatred in his heart, due to the color of my skin. He began to ask me questions like, "What's your name, where are you from and why did you come here?" I replied by asking him, "What church do you attend?" He said, "I'm a member of...!" Trust me, this association was not of God.

Now because it was a dream, I honestly don't remember word for word what he said, but God let me know that he was a member of the Ku Klux Klan.

After he answered my question, he asked me again more aggressively, "What's your name, where are you from, why did you come here?" At that point, a little fear began to fill my heart, because I knew we were in danger. So I began to pray.

Suddenly, God reminded me of the time when Peter denied Jesus. He was asked three different times, if he was one of the disciples and every single time, Peter said no. Then I heard God say, "If you deny me, I will deny you in front of my Father in Heaven!"

Immediately, the anointing fell fresh from heaven and all fear left. I answered in authority and I told him everything he wanted to know. I also let him know that I knew he was a racist and God wanted to deliver him from it.

He got so angry with me and this time he yelled at me and told me that we didn't belong there. Then he said that we needed to go back to where we came from.

At that point, I was trying to let my members know that we should get going, but they were still having such a good time and they weren't paying attention to anything I said. So then I yelled to get their attention and told them that we needed to leave right away.

As we all quickly left the building, we jumped in our vehicles to drive off, but the man met us in the parking lot. Then a couple more men rushed out of the building, hoped in their vehicles and drove off really fast. As we were getting into our vehicles, I could see up ahead that the men were parked, waiting for us to drive by the only entrance to get out of town. That's when I cried out to God for help, then I woke up.

Immediately, I went before the Lord in prayer. I asked Him why He showed me that dream. Then God let me know that in ministry, there will be times when we will teach and preach the gospel, but many will not receive. Many will show hatred and some may even persecute us, but we have to stand strong on the Word of God, because prejudice people need Jesus too, racist people need Jesus too and people with hatred in their hearts need Jesus as well!

God said, "Someone has to be bold enough. Someone has to go to the places that others don't want to go!"

Remember the night when Jesus got arrested? Peter got real angry and in defense, he grabbed a sword and cut off the ear of one of the soldiers, but what happened next? Did Jesus say, "Now, that's what you get for messing with the son of Man?" No! In the midst of a heated situation, Jesus turns to Peter and rebukes him. I find this to be very fascinating, because He didn't tell His (homeboys) disciples, "Okay, now jump 'em!" Instead, He still showed love and compassion by healing the soldier's ear, even though He knew their intent.

From this dream, I am inspired to share with you this, always love no matter what. Even if someone hurts or offends you, does you wrong, calls you out of your name, lies on you or to your face, you still have to show the love of Christ.

So many times, believers are so quick to defend themselves, have the last word or even fight to relieve some steam, but if we're not careful, we could end up out of the will of God. Isn't that the way of the world, encouraging confusion from the enemy? Always remember that love, forgiveness and compassion is the key! By implementing this in every aspect of life, God will use you for His glory.

THERE'S MINISTRY IN YOU!

I want you to take a few minutes and look back over your life. Do you see where you are now and where God has brought you from?

Surely you have a testimony and guess what? Everything that you've been through in life was all for his glory.

CHAPTER 5

Talk to God, He's Listening!

What is God saying in this season for your life? What is it that He wants you to know? Is it direction, clarity, a warning or an assignment? Whatever it is, He doesn't want you to be left in the dark, He wants you to be the first to know. If you desire to hear from God then you need to seek Him like never before and because there are many hindrances that can distract you from hearing, it's very important to be sensitive to the heart of God.

Now, communication is one of the keys to a successful relationship with God, but a lot of times, people don't want to know Him personally, they just want the blessings instead. Just like any other relationship, during prayer, we shouldn't be the only one's talking. We need to listen as well as pray. This is called intimacy with God.

GOD IS SPEAKING

In the Old Testament, God spoke through a donkey, a fiery flaming bush and He also sent Prophets to deliver a warning. This shows us that God will do whatever it takes to get our undivided attention, but many people don't understand that. So they end up putting God into a small box (hypothetically speaking), and expect Him to only speak from there. It don't work like that. Remember, He is the one and only, true all mighty God and the creator of all. So, however He wants to speak, be open to it.

Listed below are some ways God may choose to speak to you.

- God can speak through His Word (the Bible).
- God can speak through other men and woman of God.
- God can speak through music, television or radio.
- God can speak through His Holy Spirit.
- God can speak through you fasting and praying.
- God can speak through visions and dreams.
- God can speak through revelation and confirmation.

CHAPTER 6
_____

A Living Sacrifice

Over the years, my love has grown significantly for the Lord and my desire is to know Him more each day, because I know that without Him, I'm nothing. I can't even live without Him, because He's the very breath I breathe.

I finally understand the meaning of fully living for God and I've come to the realization that it's impossible to live for Him if you don't love Him. That's the secret behind it all, love. Someone reading this may ask, "What's love got to do with it?" Well the Bible tells us that if we love the Lord then we will keep His commandments. Think about it, how can someone obey a person's command if they don't have any love or respect for that person? They may start out following through, but if there's no love or respect then it's bound not to last.

The same goes for a career, it's almost impossible to be rooted for twenty years, if you absolutely hate what you do for a living. In order for something to last, there's got to be a love for that thing. The same goes for marriage and the same with God.

THERE'S MORE TO "JUST BEING SAVED"

Satan has many people thinking that as long as they believe in God or believe that Jesus died and rose again, they're saved. Truth is, confessing and believing was just the beginning to your salvation. He doesn't want you to focus on what it takes to stay saved.

Satan knows that his time is running short and God's judgment is soon to come. That's why he's trying to deceive as many people as possible. Remember, it's his job to do whatever it takes to keep us separated from God.

According to the book of Romans, in order to be saved you must confess and believe that Jesus Christ died and rose from the grave, but in order to stay saved, what do you think is required? It's going to take extreme obedience and sanctification and this is where a lot of believers fall short. If we apply the Word of God in our everyday lives, we will be filled with wisdom, knowledge and the power to live holy. Jesus is coming soon and He's coming for His perfect bride, but we must be ready. Scripture describes the body of Christ as His bride, but if we're unclean, we will miss out on His eternal reward.

Did you know that the laws of God weren't meant to control us, but to protect us? This is what the Israelites didn't understand. Even though we serve a merciful God, there are still consequences to our disobedience and the ultimate penalty is death.

Satan knows this, that's why there's so much temptation around, because the minute we're out of the will of God, is the minute we're unprotected. Remember, the devil's plan is to steal, kill and to destroy us. So let's stay in the will of God! We're safe there. You see? There's more to "just being saved."

So many people proclaim that they're saved or a Christian, yet still live a sinful life and God is not pleased.

Now I already know many people will disagree with what I'm teaching here, but I'm just a voice crying out in the wilderness. I'm just one of God's mouth pieces and I must share everything that the Lord has instructed me to say.

If you are a believer, then you must know that it's not enough to just believe, it's going to take righteousness.

GOD WANTS ALL OF YOU

In order to be free from sin, you must live a lifestyle of repentance every single day. Even if you don't think you did anything wrong, you want to be sure you're not offending the Lord in any way.

Now I'm not talking about asking God to forgive you then turning right back around and doing the exact same thing. I'm talking about repentance with a sincere heart. This means to turn away from sin completely.

God loves us even though we're not perfect, yet when we seek after His righteousness, we're perfect in Him.

All God wants is to be a part of your everyday life, but it's impossible if your temple (your body), is unclean. The devil wants you to believe that you have all the time in the world to get it right. Truth is, now is the time to get it right, because tomorrow isn't promised to anyone. When our temples are clean, His presence can dwell within us.

And he said to them all, if any man will come after me, let him deny himself, and take up his cross daily, and follow me.
-Luke 9:23

Think about the effect of what drugs can do to our physical bodies. Now what do you think it could do spiritually? This is a prime example of what sin does to us both naturally and spiritually. If we commit sin (even in our minds), it destroys us and literally separates us from God. In other words, if our temples are filled with unclean spirits, caused by sin, how can God dwell within us?

Have you ever been to someone's house and it's always kept clean? Don't you enjoy going over to spend time with them, because their house is always welcoming?

Well what if you were invited to someone's house and it was nasty? Now, I'm not talking about a few items left out here and there. What if as soon as you walked in their house, you were greeted with an unpleasant smell due to the house never being cleaned and before you entered in, you looked around and seen maggots crawling everywhere, because the trash was never taken out? You don't have to answer that, I'm pretty sure you would quickly change your mind about entering in.

Now I apologize for being so vivid, but I want you to get a visual of what God sees and how He feels when our temples are unclean.

God wants to visit you, spend time with you, and reside within you, but your temple must always be clean. When our temples are clean, it becomes a dwelling place for the Lord.

If you're someone who struggles with sin, God wants to deliver you today. So right now, I pray that whatever your struggles are, God fills you up with the Holy Ghost and gives you the simultaneous strength to overcome and be free completely, in Jesus name I pray, amen.

QUALITIES OF A SACRIFICE

God wants to take you to a higher place, but you must be willing to pick up your cross and follow Him daily. You don't have wait until you go to church to have an intimate relationship with God, you can enjoy His presence right in the comfort of your own home. Now hear me clearly, I'm not telling you that you don't need to go to church. The bible teaches us the importance of fellowship, but I am telling you that you can worship Him any day, anytime and everywhere.

What's the quality of your sacrifice?

It's time to do an evaluation check. Do you do things for God with an attitude, do you do things just to be seen or do you do things with a sincere heart all for the glory of God? Your sacrifice to the Lord should be done with the best of your ability. Listed below are just a few ways to live a sacrificial lifestyle.

1. *Withdraw from sin completely.*
   This is a sacrifice because our flesh desires to sin.

2. *Repent with a sincere heart.*
   When you ask the Lord to forgive you daily even if you believe you did nothing wrong, you are living in humility and

that's a sacrifice, because you could be doing whatever you please.

3. *Seek after the Lord daily.*
Seeking after God is a sacrifice because it takes time and diligence to learn and gain understanding.

4. *Live in humility every day.*
This is a another form of a sacrifice, because even though you are capable of making decisions on your own, it means so much to God when you are open to wisdom, commands or even constructive criticism.

5. *Purify yourself in His Word daily.*
It's one thing to read the Bible just to say you read it, but it says a lot when you actually take out the time to be edified by His Word. In other words, reading the Word of God requires quality time in His presence and once again, God honors that.

6. *Praise and worship with a sincere heart.*
This is a form of a sacrifice, because you could literally be singing and dancing to worldly music, but instead you choose to lift up holy hands to reverence God.

As you can see, you could be doing whatever you please, but when you literally take out the time to say, "Lord, I'm doing this to bless You." God honors that and remember, He rewards those who does things with a cheerful heart.

QUALITIES OF WORSHIP

Your worship shouldn't be something that's practiced only on Sundays or only when you need something from God. True worship is a lifestyle and the evidence of your relationship with Him.

Hypocrites live throughout the week as they please, then when Sunday comes, they repent for their sins, give God a praise, then give the best offering possible and think God is well pleased.

Listen, God is omnipresent, He's all knowing and He sees everything. He sees what's done in the dark and behind closed doors. He even knows your inner thoughts and your hearts desires. So whatever you find yourself doing for the Lord, be sure your temple is clean and your worship is for real.

According to Romans 12:1, we must live totally for God. We can't do what everyone else is doing just to fit in. We must glorify the Father in everything we do.

If you haven't made a commitment to live a sacrificial lifestyle for the Lord, or maybe you've made one, but you've broken it, renew your vow to Him today and do whatever you can to cherish it. You will find that God honors those who honor Him and there are many blessings and rewards for those who love Him and keeps His commandments.

God is a spirit and they that worship him must worship him in spirit and in truth.

-John 4:24

A SACRIFICIAL LIFESTYLE

*"Lord I surrender my all to you.
Everything I do is to glorify you."*

I believe that giving is the key to a sacrificial lifestyle and there are many ways you can give to God. You can give by the dedication of service, by your tithes and offering, you can also give by helping others in need, but the number one sacrifice that you can offer up before God is righteousness. It's no easy task though, that's why it's considered a sacrifice.

You must be willing to put God above all things and as a result, God will honor you.

Jesus is the ultimate sacrifice. He gave His life for you and I by shedding His precious blood. We've been purchased with a price and that price was Jesus Christ, the precious blood of the Lamb. So now we must give back by living holy and acceptable unto Him, because our bodies don't even belong to us.

This is why we need to be rooted in the Word of God daily, because it gives us the strength and endurance we need to grow in the Lord.

Remember, your new journey as a Believer is not going to be easy. In fact, it's going to require hard work, dedication and literally the sacrifice of extreme righteousness in order to make it to the finish line and that finish line is living in paradise with the Father forever.

I beseech you therefore brethren, by the mercies of God, that ye present your bodies a living sacrifice holy, acceptable unto God, which is your reasonable service.
-Romans 12:1

CHAPTER 7
_____

Activate your Faith

According to Hebrews 11:1, it tells us that faith is the substance of things hoped for and the evidence of things unseen. This means that even though we can't see faith, we still need to apply it in our everyday lives, because if we believe it then it will come to past. It's time to activate your faith and start seeing things with your spiritual eyes!

Did you know that God requires us to have faith? Hebrews 11:6 lets us know that without it, it's impossible to please God.

Always remember, faith requires work. You can't just wake up one morning and say, "I'm going to be a millionaire!" If you weren't born into wealth, there's some actions that's required.

First, you must *believe* you can, then you need to *work* towards it and finally, once you become a millionaire, you need to do what it takes to *remain* one.

Just as it took faith to believe in God, you also need it to trust in Him. Without it, you're just going through the motions of life and accepting any and everything that comes your way.

For as the body without the spirit is dead, so faith without works is dead also.

-James 2:26

THE POWER OF THE TONGUE

Whatever you're going through, it's time to take authority over it. It doesn't matter how bad it looks or how bad it actually is. You need to speak into your life and declare what thus says the Lord.

Do you know how powerful your tongue is? If you start your day out believing that it's going to be a bad day then chances are it will be. Instead, declare how you will have a blessed and prosperous day and watch how your day turns out! This means that whatever you decree, so shall it be. Now that's not saying that you're going to have a peaceful day, it just means that you will handle it according to how you want your day to be.

If sickness is among you, why mope around and complain about it? That wouldn't change anything. Instead, believe and decree that you're healed by the precious blood of the Lamb and watch God move.

It doesn't matter the level of your sickness, you could have a common cold or full blown AIDS, Jesus still wants to heal you, but you've got to believe He can. Then you need to confess it from your mouth, because whatever you say, so shall it be and finally, you would literally have to try your faith by doing something that you weren't able to do before. If you're not able to move a certain part of your body or if it hurts to move it, still move it anyway and proclaim that you are healed in Jesus name.

There has been numerous accounts where God healed my body from afflictions, so many times that I can't even count them all, but it took prayer and believing that He can.

I remember growing up as a little kid, my mom would always cover us in prayer. We didn't have health insurance, so every single time we got hurt, my mom would pray and God healed us every single time.

What if your money was getting low and you didn't have what you needed for food or bills? Should you depend on others to help you? Of course not! Why get trapped in the cycle of borrowing from an individual to pay someone else? I don't care if you're facing an eviction or a repo, stop depending on man and start depending on God!

If you're in need of a financial miracle, you must trust and believe that God will move on your behalf. Confess from your mouth that the Lord will supply all your needs and watch God move. Remember, your faith will still be tried, but if you put your trust in Him, He will work it all out for your good.

Death and Life are in the power of the tongue: and they that love it shall eat the fruit thereof.
-Proverbs 18:21

CHAPTER 8

Favor in the Storm

Recently, the Lord dealt with me concerning the signs of a natural disaster. One thing for sure, there's always going to be some sort of warning first. These signs may include a drastic change in the weather, unusual behavior in animals or you may even get that uneasy feeling letting you know something's just not right.

It doesn't matter if you pay attention to these signs or not, if a natural disaster is approaching, because of modern day technology, you can expect the weather experts to notify you to take precaution. You may be advised to relocate, take cover or stock up on supplies, such as toilet paper, batteries, candles, food, etc. Pretty much all the essentials needed for survival.

These warnings are not meant to be ignored, they're meant to be taken seriously. However, there's always that one person who believes that the storm's not going to be that bad, so they don't prepare at all. Those people are more than likely left in a sad situation that could have been avoided.

Now God gives us many warnings, yet so many people are not taking heed. These individuals come to church Sunday after Sunday, not taking the Word of God seriously. This is called operating in the spirit of disobedience.

There are two warnings that I want to focus on in my closing and the first is concerning spiritual warfare.

THE STORM IS NECESSARY FOR YOUR GROWTH

When the enemy strikes, he uses oppression to get us off track from the things of God. These attacks are also known as storms, trials and tribulations. If preparation is not taken seriously, you could find yourself in a spiritual disaster.

So many people are in spiritual warfare and don't even realize it. They're too busy trying to figure out how to make it through, instead of putting their trust in God.

Remember the story of Job? God allowed him to go through a storm and even though Job didn't understand, he still trusted that God was going to bring him out of it. When he finally came out, he was given double for his trouble.

I recently heard a testimony from a man who went through a storm. He was burned out of his house and lost everything, but God saved him and his family. In spite of what happened, this man still had the joy of the Lord and because of that, God gave him restoration.

Blessed is the man that trusteth in the Lord, and whose hope the Lord is.

-Jeremiah 17:7

    You may not understand what you're going through, but God is trying to take you to another level spiritually. Which means, you have to go through the storm. He knows that if you take heed to His instructions, when you finally come out, you will be stronger and wiser than you were before.

    When God dealt with me concerning this topic, I heard the Lord say, "The storm is necessary for your growth." Even though the devil plans to set you up and take you out, it's God who allows you to go through it.

For he shall be as a tree planted by the waters, and that spreadeth out her roots by the river, and shall not see when heat cometh, but her leaf shall be green; and shall not be careful in the year of drought, neither shall cease from yielding fruit.

-Jeremiah 17:8

WISDOM IS THE KEY TO SURVIVING ANY STORM

There's a storm coming and you can't afford to not be ready. I don't care if everything's peachy cream right now, you must take heed to the warnings. By knowing what to expect, you'll know how to prepare. For instance, if you knew that Brian was coming in town, you would keep an eye out for Brian, because you know that Brian did you wrong the last time. That's wisdom.

God knows the plans of the enemy and remember, He doesn't want you to be left in the dark. God is trying to equip you, because He knows that your weapons are not carnal. He wants to fill you up with His wisdom and knowledge needed to overcome any storm.

Listen, anytime we go through a storm our faith will be tried, but in order to overcome, we need to know how to fight effectively. Ephesians 6:10 tells us that we don't wrestle against flesh and blood but against:

1. Principalities
2. Powers
3. Rulers and darkness of this world
4. Spiritual wickedness in high places

This scripture means that our warfare are not carnal. So the only way to fight off temptations and to overcome the trials and tribulations of this world is to defeat the enemy by standing firmly on the Word of God.

Always remember that the storm is necessary for your growth. It doesn't matter if you're in a snow storm, tornado storm, or a spiritual storm, God's got it all under control and if continue to trust Him and take heed to His instructions, He will carry you through it.

CHAPTER 9

Forever His

In my previous chapter, I covered information on spiritual warfare and what you need to do to prepare for it. Now, I want to enlighten you on the times we're living in. You may or may not have heard this before, but it's true, we're living in the last days. Time is winding down and Jesus is soon to come.

Your probably thinking to yourself, "Yeah right, my great, great grandmother said the exact same thing and there's still no signs of Him yet." My comment to that is, many people feel the same way you do, they're getting weary and beginning to lose faith, but the Bible gives us comforting promises concerning the return of our Lord and savior, Jesus Christ. In fact, many of the biblical prophecies have already come to pass. This is why we can't afford to be caught up in the world, because we could really miss God.

Have you ever thought about what happens to someone after they die or have you ever considered what will take place after you die? Even though this is a tough topic to ponder upon, everyone seems to have their own opinion or belief on what happens after life. Some people believe in reincarnation, while others believe they'll become some sort of angel, but to cut down all the confusion and wishful thinking, I prefer to believe what the Bible says.

When Jesus returns, some will be living and some will be in the grave, but to sum it all up, everyone will be judged and if your name is written in the Lamb's Book of Life, you'll spend eternity in the kingdom of God, if not, you'll be cast away into everlasting fire.

As I'm writing this chapter, I'm literally in tears, because there will be so many people who will miss out on the promises of God. So please don't take this warning for granted. Jesus is coming soon and you must be ready!

Take a look at your life right now and acknowledge everything that God may not be pleased with. Be sure to repent with a sincere heart and turn away from your sins.

WHEN JESUS COMES

One night I had a dream that I was in the midst of a king who was seated on a throne. Due to His brightness that illuminated all around Him, I couldn't make out His face, but I knew it was Jesus. In the midst of Him were sheep and goats. On His right hand side were thousands upon thousands of sheep and on His left, were thousands upon thousands of goats. I don't remember word for word what was said, but I knew they were all being judged. He told the sheep on His right that they were going to be rewarded and dwell in His kingdom forever, but to the goats, He told them that they were going to be punished and cast away. The sheep were rejoicing, but the goats were sad and confused. I could hear them murmuring amongst themselves as they questioned the King. The King told them they had their chance and now it was too late, then He sent them away. Immediately, I woke up crying and praying to God, because I felt every emotion from every individual.

Later that day, I shared the dream with a close friend of mine and she encouraged me to read Matthew 25: 31-46, because it explains how the Lord will separate the sheep from the goats. When I read it for myself, I was astonished, because everything that was in my dream was written in the Bible.

It tells us that when Jesus returns, He's coming to judge. All nations will be gathered before Him and will be separated. His sheep will be on His right side and the goats will be on His left. The goats are the ones who deliberately disobeyed and denied Him. They will be cast into everlasting fire, but the sheep,

His sheep, the ones who were obedient, the ones who were faithful and the ones who kept His commandments, will inherit His kingdom throughout all eternity.

Then shall the King say unto them on his right hand, Come, ye blessed of my Father, inherit the kingdom prepared for you from the foundation of the world.
                                                    -*Matthew 25:34*

After reading those scriptures, the Lord let me know that He is not pleased with the wickedness in the world, and before the wrath of God comes, He's going to redeem His sheep. So get ready, get ready, get ready, our Savior is soon to come. We can't even afford to be lukewarm, that's not going to cut it. We're either going to be hot or cold and I suggest you be hot and on fire with the Holy Ghost. Woe unto those who have heard, but did not receive.

TIME TO WAKE UP!

If you're curious about when the Lord will return, you won't get that information here. The Bible declares that no one knows the day or the hour, not even the angels in heaven, only our heavenly Father knows. However, the Word of God gives us insight on what to expect on that glorious day and what we need to do to prepare for it. Can you imagine what will take place when Jesus returns?

As that day approaches, we need to continually wait patiently on the Lord. The Bible says that every knee shall bow and every tongue shall confess that He is Lord. That's why it's so important to be ready, because we cannot afford to miss God.

Be ye therefore ready also: for the Son of man cometh at an hour when ye think not.
-Luke 12:40

Many people are spiritually dead or asleep, but it's time to wake up. Jesus is coming soon, yet many people are unaware or still not ready.

According to John 3:29, the Body of Christ is His bride and Jesus is our bridegroom. So we must literally look at His coming as our wedding day. We should also look at our lives as the wedding dress.

Now just as a bride protects her dress in preparation for her wedding, we must also protect our garments (our temples), for the coming Messiah.

That he might present it to himself a glorious church, not having spot, or wrinkle, or any such thing; but that it should be holy and without blemish.
-Ephesians 5:27

Jesus is coming soon and it's my responsibility as an ambassador of the Lord to share with you the insights of the times we're living in.

A young lady once asked me, "How is it possible not to sin at all?" I replied by telling her, if she focuses on pleasing God and living holy, she won't have to worry about trying not to sin. See when you have a desire not to sin, your relationship with the Lord will grow and God will give you the power needed to resist the devil, including all of his temptations. That's how you can live a sin free life.

WHO WILL ENTER THE KINGDOM OF GOD?

The Bible says that the righteous will scarcely enter in. So what does this mean? It means that it doesn't exclude any elders, pastors, preachers, prophets or teachers. If you have a calling over your life or if you're someone in high authority, it still doesn't matter, the devil is not going to make it easy for you just because of your position or title. He's going to do everything in his power to get you to fall short from the glory of God. However, the Bible is still clear on what will take place when Jesus returns. It says that every knee will bow and every tongue will confess that Jesus is Lord. This is why it's so important to be ready when the Lord cracks the sky. It's very sad, but everyone won't make it into the kingdom of God, even a lot of Christians will miss out on His eternal promises.

Nor thieves, nor covetous, nor drunkards, nor revilers, nor extortioners, shall inherit the kingdom of God.
-1 Corinthians 6:10

I'M GAY, WILL I MAKE IT IN?

Now what I'm about to say here will offend many people, but I pray that if it does, let it convict you in such a way to get it right with God. A lot of times, the reason why a discussion like this normally gets offensive is because now-a-days people don't like to hear the truth. So what ends up happening is, people who know better get intimidated and ends up sugar coating the truth all for the sake of pleasing others. I'm telling you right now, I can't afford to sugar coat anything, because I'm held accountable for everything I say and everything I do. Therefore, the Bible clearly says that the unrighteous will not inherit the kingdom of God. This includes all homosexuals or anyone who struggles with sexual sins.

Or do you not know that the unrighteous will not inherit the kingdom of God? Do not be deceived: neither the sexually immoral, nor idolaters, nor adulterers, nor men who practice homosexuality,

- 1 Corinthians 6:9

For you may be sure of this, that everyone who is sexually immoral or impure, or who is covetous (that is, an idolater), has no inheritance in the kingdom of Christ and God.

-Ephesians 5:5

Recently, God dealt with me concerning the coming judgment of the Lord. He revealed to me that it wasn't for the righteous, but for those who deliberately disobeyed.

Judgment is coming and if you do not receive what I am saying before Jesus returns or before you take your last breath then you will be held accountable for every un-repented sin.

In Conclusion

Many people have strayed away from God. They once knew Him, but they've allowed the devil to deceive them into believing something else. Their hearts grew cold towards God and it seems like no matter what someone says to them, they've made up their minds, they're going to believe what they want. Also, many people don't believe at all or never even heard the gospel. For those reasons alone is why this book was birthed. God put it on my heart to do what I can to lead as many people into paradise, but it still stands to be true, everyone will not receive, but I pray you receive, because God has great things in stored for you, including everlasting life.

As you can see, there's so much more to just believing. God not only wants you saved, set free and delivered so that you can inherit His kingdom, He also wants to use you to lead others as well.

If you have received Jesus Christ as your personal savior, I also pray that you be filled with the Holy Ghost, which is the spirit of God, because His spirit will guide and protect you as well as give you power to overcome every obstacle in life. With His spirit, there is no such thing as dabbling in sin, but being fully equipped with everything you need to overcome in these last and evil days.

As you heard it many times before, the earth we live in today is not promised to us tomorrow. Therefore, we must continue to strive and be ready for the coming Messiah.

I pray that this book was encouraging to you, because let's admit it, when life gets us down, sometimes we just want to give up and throw in the towel, but we got to hang in there and wait patiently on the Lord.

The Bible tells us that if we endure for a night, our joy will come in the morning. It also tells us that when all these things have come to pass, look up towards the sky because our redemption is soon to come.

Listen, the spirit of the anti-christ is rising up and deceiving many people like never before, especially the believers, but it's so important to hang in there, keep your faith and continue to strive.

Remember, the purpose of your salvation is not just to be called a Christian, but to be redeemed by our Lord and savior when He comes.

NOTES TO REMEMBER

CHAPTER 1: A CALL FOR REPENTANCE

- When we turn from sin and live holy, we are more open to hear from God directly. There are so many things that God wants to reveal to us, but if our lives don't line up with the Word of God then it will be very difficult to hear from Him.
- Acts 16:31 tells us that if we believe in the Lord Jesus Christ, we shall be saved. Romans 10:9 tells us that if anyone calls on the name of Jesus they shall be saved. If you haven't received Jesus Christ as your personal savior, then you haven't received the gift of eternal life. If you want to be free from the bondages of sin, then give your heart to Jesus right now.
- Steps to Salvation:
  1. Acknowledge that you are a sinner.

NOTES TO REMEMBER

2. Believe that Jesus is the son of God.
3. Repent with a sincere heart and ask God to forgive you of all your sins.
4. Accept Jesus as your Lord and Savior.
5. Confess Jesus as your Lord and Savior.

- Congratulations!!! If you said the sinner's prayer on pg.28 with a sincere heart, then God has heard your cry and Jesus is now your Lord and personal Savior. Now that you have accepted Jesus Christ into your heart, you have also accepted the gift of eternal life.

CHAPTER 2: I'M SAVED! NOW WHAT?

- Now that you are a believer, one of the first steps to growing in your walk with Christ is to read your Bible daily. This is the number one way you can actually connect with God personally.

NOTES TO REMEMBER

- Just as often as we open our mouths to talk to our colleagues, family members or friends, it is very important to open our mouths to pray daily. By doing so, this strengthens your prayer life as well as builds your relationship with God.
- One of the first things you must understand is that God does not want religion from you, only a relationship.
- Be sure to keep your mind focused on the Lord and dedicate yourself in worship and prayer. As a result, your relationship will grow stronger in Him.

CHAPTER 3: DELIVERED FROM DARKNESS

- God has called us to a higher place in Him. Unfortunately, there are some

NOTES TO REMEMBER

things that we feel as though we can't let go of and this is where we give the enemy authority for the hindrances in our lives.
- Remember John 10:10 says that the enemy comes to steal, kill and to destroy us.
- Overcome backsliding by standing on the Word of God with love, prayer, open confession and worship.
- God has given you the ultimate power to defeat the enemy and that power is the Word of God.
- You can't just proclaim that you're a believer, yet do whatever you want to do. You must also live according to the Word of God in preparation for the coming of the Lord.

NOTES TO REMEMBER

CHAPTER 4: A NEW BEGINNING

- Renew your mind by practicing the SMC system daily. Be sure to acknowledge every thought and identify where it's coming from.
- By following this system, you'll be able to recognize the enemy when he speaks and hear God's voice more clearly.
- To walk in your calling means to walk in extreme obedience.
- If you woke up this morning then there's an assignment that you need to fulfill.
- God has a divine plan and it's been laid out for you, but if you're not operating in the heart of God, you will not be able to walk into your calling as effectively.
- Everything that you've been through in life is all for His glory.

NOTES TO REMEMBER

CHAPTER 5: TALK TO GOD, HE'S LISTENING!

- God can speak through His Word, through other men and woman of God, through music, television or radio, through His Holy Spirit, through you fasting and praying, through your dreams and visions, and through revelation and confirmation.
- If you want to hear from God, you have to be sensitive to Him.

CHAPTER 6: A LIVING SACRIFICE

- According to the book of Romans, in order to be saved, you must confess and believe that Jesus Christ died and rose from the grave, but in order to stay saved, do you remember what is required? It's going to take extreme obedience and sanctification and this is where a lot of believers fall short.

NOTES TO REMEMBER

- If you're a believer, then you must remember, it's not enough to just believe, it's going to take righteousness to be saved.
- God loves us even though we're not perfect, yet when we seek after His righteousness, we're perfect in Him.

- Qualities of a Sacrifice:
1. Withdraw from all sin.
2. Repent with a sincere heart.
3. Seek after the Lord daily.
4. Live in humility every day.
5. Purify yourself in His Word daily.
6. Bring sacrifices of praise and worship unto the Lord with a sincere heart.
7. And whatever you do, be found doing it with a sincere heart.

- God is omnipresent, He's all knowing and He sees everything. He sees what's done in the dark or behind closed doors.

NOTES TO REMEMBER

He even knows your inner thoughts and your hearts desires. So whatever you find yourself doing, do it for the Lord.
- Be sure your temple is clean and your worship is for real.
- Remember, your new journey as a Christian is not going to be easy. In fact, it's going to require a lot of work. It's going to take a sacrificial lifestyle of extreme righteousness in order to make it to the finish line. That finish line is with Jesus Christ in paradise for all eternity.

CHAPTER 7: ACTIVATE YOUR FAITH

- According to Hebrews 11:6, God requires us to have faith, because without it, it's impossible to please Him.
- Always remember, faith requires work.

NOTES TO REMEMBER

- Remember, your faith will always be tried, but if you put your trust in God, He will work it all out for your good.

CHAPTER 8: FAVOR IN THE STORM

- When the enemy strikes, he uses oppression to get us off track from the things of God. These attacks are also known as storms, trials and tribulations. If preparation is not taken seriously, you could find yourself in a spiritual disaster.
- Preparation is necessary before any storm, that's why it's important to always be ready.

CHAPTER 9: FOREVER HIS

- Jesus is coming soon and no man knows the day or the hour, that's why we must be ready because the unrighteous will not inherit the kingdom of God.

Daily Prayers

I've implemented some prayers to help lead you into prayer. A lot of times people are too afraid to pray, because they feel like they don't know what to say. Well, there is no wrong way to pray. All it takes is honesty with a sincere heart. God hears every prayer. Anytime you feel you're under attack, facing some kind of spiritual warfare or maybe you need God to move on your behalf, just pray and God will hear your cry.

PRAYER FOR SALVATION

Dear Jesus, please forgive me for all of my sins. I believe that you are the Son of God and you shed your precious blood for me. Your Word says that if I confess that you are Lord and believe that God raised you from the dead, then I shall be saved. So right now, I confess that you are my Lord and Savior and I believe that you conquered the grave when you died and rose from the dead. Now according to your Word, I am saved. So Lord I ask that you transform my life. Teach me how to live holy and acceptable to you and create in me a clean heart in Jesus name I pray, amen.

INVITATION FOR THE HOLY SPIRIT

Oh Lord, I worship you and I give you all the honor and all the praise. You alone are worthy. Let your glory fill this place. In Jesus name, hallelujah amen.

PRAYER FOR HEALING

Heal me O' God. Lord you said in your Word that by your strips, I am healed so I decree and declare that I am healed. Satan, the blood of Jesus is against you and I command you to flee out of my body. I command all pain and all diseases to go right now in the mighty name of Jesus. I pray for a full healing. In Jesus name, Amen.

PRAYER AGAINST HINDERING SPIRITS

Father, I thank you for honoring my prayer by giving me the power to cast down every demonic force and every stronghold that's been assigned to me, my family, my finances, my health, my children, my transportation and even my job. I come against all hindering spirits in the mighty name of Jesus Christ. I cancel every assignment that is a hindrance to my life. In Jesus name I pray, Amen.

PRAYER FOR FORGIVENESS

Father, I know that I've done wrong and I no longer desire to be out of your Will. I'm sorry for what I've done, please forgive me. Wash me so that I can be clean before you. Give me a new mind so that I can have a new way of thinking. Give me the strength and the power I need to overcome the temptations of all sin. Thank you Father for forgiving me in Jesus name I pray, Amen.

PRAYER FOR PEACE

Father, I am praying for peace, because I don't want to worry or fear anymore. All I want to do is trust you, because I know that if I put my faith in you, everything will be okay. So God, as I bless your name, I give you praise for the peace in my mind. Lord I thank you for the peace in my health, and in spite of what the doctors say, I am healed in Jesus name. Lord I thank you for the peace in my finances, because, I trust that you will provide for us. Lord, thank you for the peace in my household and peace in my marriage. Lord I thank you for the peace in my _____. In Jesus name I pray, Amen.

PRAYER FOR WISDOM

Father, according to Matthew 7:7, you said in your word that if I ask, it shall be given. If I seek, I shall find and if I knock, the door shall be opened unto me and because I know that all revelation and knowledge comes from you, Lord I'm asking and seeking for your wisdom. Lord please give me the wisdom I need for _____. In Jesus name I pray, Amen.

PRAYER FOR FAVOR

Father, please grant me the favor I need to _____. I know that I can't do this on my own, but God I need you. What I'm asking for requires something that I don't have, but I have faith and I believe that you will move on my behalf. Lord I pray that you honor this prayer and let your will be done. In Jesus name I pray, Amen.

PRAYER FOR ENDURANCE

Father, it's not easy and I feel like giving up, but God I know that if you're allowing me to go through this, then you know that I can come out of it. So I ask that you give me the strength I need to overcome this. I ask that you give me peace in the midst of my storm. Lord I pray that in spite of what I'm going through, you keep me. Lord keep my mind, so that I won't worry, fear or have any doubt. Lord help me to keep my mind focused on you and not to focus on my current situation. Lord I know that this is only for a season, so while I'm going through _____, I want to praise your name. I thank you in advance, because I already know, you have greater in stored for me. In Jesus name I pray, Amen.

PRAYER FOR SPOUSE

Father, I pray that you move on my (husband's/wife's) behalf. Lord whatever it is that they are facing or going through, I ask that you carry them through it. I pray that you give them the desires of his/her heart as well as lead and guide him/her in your perfect Will. Give him/her the strength, power and revelation he/she needs to grow spiritually. In Jesus name I pray, Amen.

PRAYER FOR PROTECTION

Father I pray that you protect me as I go about my day. Place a hedge of protection around my family, health, finances and everything I own or come in contact with. Lord I ask that you release your angels to protect my household even while we're sleeping. Thank you for your protection. In Jesus name I pray, Amen.

PRAYER FOR DELIVERANCE

Lord I know that I've done wrong which is unpleasing in your sight, but father I pray that you forgive me. I pray that you cleanse me and deliver me from anything that is hindering me from living in your perfect Will. In Jesus name I pray, Amen.

Dear Friend,

Thank you so much for taking the time to read this book. I pray it was a blessing to you. The purpose of this book is to strengthen the body of Christ, win souls for the kingdom of God and to prepare everyone for the coming of the Lord. If you have been impacted in any way after reading this book, please share your testimony on my website. We want to hear from you.

If you liked what you read and want to support this mission, please visit my website to learn more at: www.shavonneandrews.com. Thank you and God bless you.

Sincerely,

Shavonne Andrews
Your Sister in Christ

LEARN HOW TO WRITE AND SELF-PUBLISH YOUR OWN BOOK

In this book, you will learn…

- ✓ How to write your book in any season
- ✓ How to overcome writer's block
- ✓ Secrets to completing your book

To order your copy today or to attend an upcoming workshop, please visit: www.shavonneandrews.com.

www.ingramcontent.com/pod-product-compliance
Lightning Source LLC
Chambersburg PA
CBHW061946070426
42450CB00007BA/1063